MW01059661

Devotions for Eucharistic Holy Hour

A Redemptorist Pastoral Publication
Compiled by Brother Daniel Korn, C.Ss.R.

Liguori

ONE LIGUORI DRIVE
LIGUORI MO 63057-9999

Imprimi Potest:
Richard Thibodeau, C.Ss.R.
Provincial, Denver Province
The Redemptorists

Imprimatur:
Most Reverend Michael J. Sheridan
Auxiliary Bishop, Archdiocese of St. Louis

ISBN 0-7648-0515-0
Library of Congress Catalog Card Number: 99-62946

Except where noted, Scripture quotations are from the *New
Revised Standard Version of the Bible*, © 1989 by the
Division of Christian Education of the National Council of
Churches of Christ in the USA. Used with permission. All rights
reserved.

"Prayer of the Forty-Seventh International Eucharistic Congress"
is reprinted by permission of *L'Osservatore Romano*.

Excerpts from the English translation of *Holy Communion and
Worship of the Eucharist Outside of Mass*, © 1974, International
Commission on English in the Liturgy, Inc (ICEL). All rights
reserved.

Selected Scripture quotations are taken from the *Christian Community Bible*, Catholic Pastoral Edition, © 1995, Liguori Publi-
cations. All rights reserved.

To order, call 1-800-325-9521. *http://www.liguori.org*

Cover design by Lynne Condellone

I dedicate this book in
loving memory of
Brother Florian Shalowski, C.Ss.R.,
who by his example taught me the value of
eucharistic adoration.

Contents

Adoration of the Eucharist

Throughout the Catholic world, devotion to the Blessed Sacrament is increasing. Perpetual adoration groups are forming in dioceses throughout our country, and parishes are selecting weekly or monthly hours for adoration and prayer before the exposed Eucharist.

Eucharistic devotion is time spent in common or private prayer before the Blessed Sacrament, exposed for our adoration outside of the celebration of the Mass. In his *Letter on the 750th Anniversary of the Feast of Corpus Christi,* Pope John Paul says, "Remaining in silence before the Blessed Sacrament, it is Christ totally and really present whom we discover, whom we adore, and with whom we are in contact."

This booklet is an encouragement for those who feel drawn to eucharistic devotion. These prayers help us enter into disciple-friendship with Jesus Christ. His presence in this sacrament of the altar is his gift to us. In the Gospel of John, Jesus speaks to us, saying, "I am the bread of life. Whoever comes to me will never be hungry, and whoever believes in me will never be thirsty" (John 6:35). Time spent in adoration before the Blessed Sacrament is one way for us to nourish our spiritual life. Jesus will feed our hungry hearts and take away our thirst. As we spend time in silent reflection on the Word of God prayed in his eucharistic presence, our minds and hearts open to the inner meaning of the gospel. This sacred time spent in the presence of Christ will help us live the gospel in our daily lives.

All adoration of the Eucharist stems from one source, the sacrifice of the Mass.

Pope John Paul II says, "Prayer of adoration in the presence of the Blessed Sacrament unites the faithful with the Paschal Mystery; it enables them to share in Christ's sacrifice of which the Eucharist is the permanent Sacrament" *(Letter...Corpus Christi).*

In the celebration of the Mass, we enter into the mystery of Christ's dying and rising. We gather to hear the Word of God proclaimed in Scripture, we receive instruction in the homily, we make intercessions, and we offer bread and wine to be transformed into the Body and Blood of Jesus Christ. We receive the Lord in holy Communion and are sent forth to be his living presence in the world.

Traditional forms of eucharistic adoration—processions, Benediction of the Blessed Sacrament, perpetual adoration, and visits to the Blessed Sacrament—are practices familiar to many Catholics. We appreciate both the tradition of these devotions and the liturgical renewal of the Second Vatican Council, which gave us the beautiful restored ritual. The new emphasis is on the communal celebration of the Eucharist and on the continuation of that celebration as we live out the mystery of Christ's presence in our lives.

For those who desire to enter into a close relationship with Jesus in the Eucharist, much can be learned from sitting at the feet of the Master in silent prayer. Prayer books and favorite devotional prayers are helpful but not an end in themselves. They only lead us to the prayer of silence in the presence of Christ.

Eucharistic adoration is not a replacement for the communal celebration of the Eucharist. (*See* Church Teaching on the Eucharist, *page 75.*) We also should make serious attempts to educate ourselves about the Eucharist by reading and by participating in eucharistic and liturgical seminars and conferences.

"Come to me, all you that are weary and are carrying heavy burdens, and I will give you rest" (Matthew 11:28). Here is an invitation from Christ for those who seek an intimate relationship with him. In his eucharistic presence you will find rest and strength for the journey. After thirty-three years of living the religious life, I have found silent adoration before the Eucharist to be a prayer that heals and encourages me in living the gospel. When I was in formation, an old Brother would often tell me, "Go to the Master Jesus. He is present in the Blessed Sacrament waiting for your visit."

Through your eucharistic devotion, may you come to know the Lord in new and deeper ways.

Rite of Benediction

Public Adoration of the Blessed Sacrament

During the exposition there should be prayers, songs, and readings to direct the attention of the faithful to the worship of Christ the Lord. To encourage a prayerful spirit, there should be readings from Scripture with a homily or brief exhortations to develop a better understanding of the eucharistic mystery. It is also desirable for the people to respond to the Word of God by singing and to spend some periods of time in religious silence.

The Rites of the Catholic Church,
Vol. I (The Rites)

Rite of Eucharistic Exposition and Benediction

Exposition

While the assembly sings a eucharistic song (see pages 67-74), the presider approaches the sanctuary and makes an appropriate reverence. He then removes the sacrament from the tabernacle and puts it in a monstrance, which is usually placed on the altar. He then incenses the Blessed Sacrament.

A reading from Scripture is proclaimed from the lectern and is followed by a period of silence. The presider should be seated.

Choose either a lectionary reading
or a eucharistic Scripture passage.

LECTIONARY READINGS

The following are suggested lectionary readings. (The numbers in brackets match the red numbers in the *Lectionary for Mass*.)

[49] John 21:1-9

[53] John 14:1-2
[281] John 12:44-50
[360] Matthew 5:13-16
[464] Luke 11:5-13

EUCHARISTIC SCRIPTURE PASSAGES

Choose a passage from Scripture Passages for Meditation before the Eucharist, pages 16-22.

HOMILY

Next is a homily, followed by a period of silence.

In its document *Solemn Exposition of the Holy Eucharist*, the National Conference of Catholic Bishops has this to say about other devotions and liturgies:

> Other devotions, although good and commendable, take attention away to a different object and should therefore be assigned to another time, either before or after exposition and benediction of the blessed sacrament.

Sometimes it is the practice to celebrate the Liturgy of the Hours (see pages 23-42) before or after the rite of benediction.

Benediction

After the silence, the presider returns to the altar and incenses the sacrament while a eucharistic hymn is sung (see pages 67-74 for suggested hymns). Then while standing facing the people, he says or sings the following or one of several other optional prayers.

> Lord Jesus Christ, you have given us this
>   sacrament
> in remembrance of your suffering and
>   death.
> May our worship of this sacrament of your
>   body and blood
> help us to experience the salvation you have
>   won for us
> and the peace of the kingdom where you live
> with the Father and the Holy Spirit,
> one God, forever and ever.
> All: Amen

The Rites Vol. I.

The presider takes the monstrance and, in silence, makes the Sign of the Cross over those assembled. After the benediction with the sacrament, the Eucharist is immediately replaced in the tabernacle.

The presider then makes the appropriate reverence in the sanctuary and returns to the sacristy while the assembly sings an acclamation or hymn.

If no hymn is sung, the Canticle of Simeon may be recited as the presider leaves the altar.

CANTICLE OF SIMEON
All: Now, Master, let your servant go in peace, for my eyes have seen your salvation, which you prepared in sight of all the peoples, a light for revelation to the Gentiles, and glory for your people Israel.

Glory to the Father, the Son, and the Holy Spirit, both now and forever. Amen

Scripture Passages for Meditation Before the Eucharist

The following Scripture passages, chosen for their strong eucharistic themes, may be used for meditation. As you select one and read it slowly, let it direct you into silent prayer before the Lord.

We have a great High Priest, Jesus, the Son of God, who has entered heaven. Let us, then, hold fast to the faith we profess. Our high priest is not indifferent to our weaknesses, for he was tempted in every way just as we are, yet without sinning. Let us, then, with confidence approach God, the giver of grace; we

will obtain mercy and, through his favor, help
in due time.
Hebrews 4:14-16, Christian Community Bible (CCB)

He is the image of the unseen God,
and for all creation he is the firstborn,
for in him all things were created,
in heaven and on earth,
visible and invisible:
thrones, rulers, authorities, powers…
All was made through him and for him.
He is before all
and all things hold together in him.
And he is the head of his body, the Church,
for he is the first, the first raised from the
    dead
that he may be the first in everything,
for God was pleased to let fullness dwell
    in him.
Through him God willed to reconcile all
    things to himself,
and through him, through his blood shed
    on the cross,
God establishes peace,
on earth as in heaven.

Colossians 1:15-20, CCB

Everything seems to me as nothing compared with the knowledge of Christ Jesus, my Lord. For his sake I have let everything fall away and I now consider all as garbage, if instead I may gain Christ. May I be found in him, without merit or holiness of my own for having fulfilled the Law, but with the holiness which comes through faith in Christ, the holiness given by God which depends on faith in Christ Jesus.

May I know him and experience the power of his resurrection and share in his sufferings and become like him in his death, and attain through this, God willing, the resurrection from the dead! I do not believe I have already reached the goal, nor do I consider myself perfect, but I press on till I possess Christ Jesus, since I have been pursued by him. No, brothers and sisters, I do not claim to have claimed the prize yet. I say only this: forgetting what is behind me, I race forward and run toward the goal, my eyes on the prize to which God has called us from above in Christ Jesus. Let all of us who claim to be perfect have the same way of thinking, but if there is something on which you differ, God will make it clear to you. In the meantime, let us hold on to what we have attained.

Philippians 3:8-16, CCB

This is the tradition of the Lord that I received and that in my turn I have handed on to you; the Lord Jesus, on the night that he was delivered up, took bread and, after giving thanks, broke it, saying, "This is my body which is broken for you; do this in memory of me." In the same manner, taking the cup after the supper, he said, "This cup is the new Covenant in my blood. Whenever you drink it, do it in memory of me." So, then, whenever you eat of this bread and drink from this cup, you are proclaiming the death of the Lord until he comes.

1 Corinthians 11:23-26, CCB

I am the bread of life. Though your ancestors ate the manna in the desert, they died. But here you have the bread which comes from heaven so that you may eat of it and not die.

I am the living bread which has come from heaven; whoever eats of this bread will live forever. The bread I shall give is my flesh and I will give it for the life of the world.

The Jews were arguing among themselves, "How can this man give us (his) flesh to eat?" So Jesus replied, "Truly, I say to you, if you do not eat the flesh of the Son of Man and drink his blood, you have no life in you. He who eats my flesh and drinks my blood lives with eternal life and I will raise him up on the last day.

My flesh is really food and my blood is drink. He who eats my flesh and drinks my blood, lives in me and I in him. Just as the Father, who is life, sent me and I have life from the Father, so he who eats me will have life from me. This is the bread which came from heaven; unlike that of your ancestors, who ate and later died. He who eats this bread will live forever.

John 6:48-58, CCB

How lovely are your rooms,
O Lord of hosts!
My soul yearns, pines,
for the courts of the Lord.
My heart and my flesh
cry out for the living God.

Even the sparrow finds a home,
and the swallow a nest
where she may lay her young,
at your altars, O Lord of hosts,
my King and my God!

Happy are those who live in your house,
continually singing your praise!
Happy the pilgrims whom you strengthen,
to make the ascent to you.

As they pass through the Valley
they make it a place of springs,
the early rain covers it with blessings.
They go from strength to strength
till they appear before God in Zion.
O Lord of hosts, hear my prayer;
give ear, O God of Jacob!
Look upon our shield, O God;
look upon the face of your anointed!

One day in your courts is better
than a thousand elsewhere.
I would rather be left at the threshold
in the house of my God
than to dwell in the tents of the wicked.

For the Lord God is a sun and a shield;
he bestows favor and glory.
The Lord withholds no good thing
from those who walk in uprightness.
O Lord of hosts,
blessed are those who trust in you.

Psalm 84, CCB

I am the bread of life; he who comes to me shall never be hungry, and he who believes in me shall never be thirsty. Nevertheless, as I said, you refuse to believe, even when you have seen. Yet, all that the Father gives me will come to me, and whoever comes to me, I shall not turn away. For I have come from heaven, not to do my own will, but the will of the One who sent me.

And the will of him who sent me is that I lose nothing of what he has given me, but instead that I raise it up on the last day. This is the will of the Father, that whoever sees the Son and believes in him shall live with eternal life; and I will raise him up on the last day.

John 6:35-40, CCB

Liturgy of the Hours

(*The following psalms are taken from the* Christian Community Bible.)

Morning Prayer

For Mondays, Wednesdays, and Fridays

V. God, come to my assistance.
R. Lord, make haste to help me.
V. Glory to the Father, the Son, and the Holy Spirit,
R. Both now and forever. Amen

Hymn

(Optional. See pages 67-74.)

PSALM 113

Antiphon: The one who eats my flesh and drinks my blood will live in me, says the Lord.

Praise, O servants of the Lord,
praise the name of the Lord!
Blessed be the name of the Lord
now and forever!

From eastern lands to the western islands,
may the name of the Lord be praised!

The Lord is exalted over the nations,
his glory above the heavens.
Who is like the Lord our God,
who sits enthroned on high,
but also bends down to see
on earth as in heaven?

He lifts up the poor from the dust
and the needy from the ash heap.

He makes them sit with princes,
with rulers of his people.

He gives a home to the barren woman,
and makes her a joyful mother.
Praise the Lord!

Glory to the Father, the Son, and the
Holy Spirit, both now and forever. Amen

ANTIPHON

SCRIPTURE READING
The reading can be taken from the liturgy of the
day or from one of the gospel readings from the
Scripture passages on pages 16-23.

SILENT REFLECTION

CANTICLE OF ZECHARIAH
(Luke 1:68-79)

Blessed be the Lord God of Israel, for he has looked
favorably on his people and redeemed them.

He has raised up a mighty savior for us in the house of his servant David, as he spoke through the mouth of his holy prophets from of old, that we would be saved from our enemies and from the hand of all who hate us.

Thus he has shown the mercy promised to our ancestors, and has remembered his holy covenant, the oath that he swore to our ancestor Abraham, to grant us that we, being rescued from the hands of our enemies, might serve him without fear, in holiness and righteousness before him all our days.

And you, child, will be called the prophet of the Most High; for you will go before the Lord to prepare his ways, to give knowledge of salvation to his people by the forgiveness of their sins.

By the tender mercy of our God, the dawn from on high will break upon us, to give light to those who sit in darkness and in the shadow of death, to guide our feet into the way of peace.

Glory to the Father, the Son, and the Holy Spirit, both now and forever. Amen

PRAYERS OF INTERCESSION

Lord, hear the prayer I offer for those
who are in need.

Lord, I pray for the Church. May it always be
faithful to the gospel.

Lord, remember those who are without shelter,
food, and meaningful employment.

Lord, keep all those I love in your loving care
this day.

(Pray now for your own intentions.)

THE LORD'S PRAYER

CLOSING PRAYER

Almighty God, you have brought us to another day.
We give you praise and glory. Fill our hearts with
love for you, increase our faith, and in your mercy
protect us through this day.

We ask this through our Lord Jesus Christ, your Son,
who lives and reigns with you and the Holy Spirit,
one God, forever and ever. Amen

(See Seasonal Prayers, pages 43-47, for an alternative prayer proper to the season of the year.)

Morning Prayer

For Tuesdays, Thursdays, and Saturdays

V. God, come to my assistance.
R. Lord, make haste to help me.
V. Glory to the Father, the Son, and the Holy Spirit,
R. Both now and forever. Amen

Hymn

(Optional. See pages 67-74.)

PSALM 111
Antiphon: Jesus had always loved those who were his in the world, but now he showed how perfect his love was.

I thank the Lord with all my heart
in the council of the just, in the assembly.

The works of the Lord are great
and pondered by all who delight in them.

Glorious and majestic are his deeds,
his righteousness endures forever.
He lets us remember his wondrous deeds;
the Lord is merciful and kind.

Always mindful of his covenant,
he provides food for those who fear him.
He shows his people the power of his arm
by giving them the lands of other nations.

The works of his hands are faithful and just,
trustworthy are all his precepts,
ordained to last forever,
bearers of truth and uprightness.

He has sent his people deliverances
and made with them a covenant forever.
His holy name is to be revered!
The fear of the Lord is the beginning of wisdom;
prudent are those who live by his precepts.
To him belongs everlasting praise.

Glory to the Father, the Son, and the
Holy Spirit, both now and forever. Amen

ANTIPHON

(See pages 25-27 for Scripture, Silent Reflection, Canticle, Prayers of Intercession, the Lord's Prayer, *and* Closing Prayer.*)*

Morning Prayer

For Sundays

V. God, come to my assistance.
R. Lord, make haste to help me.
V. Glory to the Father, the Son, and the Holy Spirit,
R. Both now and forever. Amen

Hymn

(Optional. See pages 67-74.)

PSALM 63, CCB
Antiphon: I will praise your name forever, Lord.

O God, you are my God, it is you I seek;
for you my body longs and my soul thirsts,
as a dry and weary land without water.

Thus have I gazed upon you in the
sanctuary, to see your power and your glory.
Your love is better than life,
my lips will glorify you.

I will bless you as long as I live,
lift up my hands and call on your name.
As with the richest food my soul will feast;
my mouth will praise you with joyful lips.

Glory to the Father, the Son, and the
Holy Spirit, both now and forever. Amen

ANTIPHON

(See pages 25-27 for Scripture, Silent Reflection,
Canticle, Prayers of Intercession, the Lord's Prayer,
and Closing Prayer.*)*

Midday Prayer

V. God, come to my assistance.
R. Lord, make haste to help me.
V. Glory to the Father, the Son, and the Holy Spirit,
R. Both now and forever. Amen

PSALM 138
(Psalm 84, pages 21-22, may be used instead of Psalm 138.)

Antiphon: The bread that I shall give is my flesh for the life of the world.

I thank you, O Lord, with all my heart,
for you have heard the word of my lips.
I sing your praise in the presence of the gods.

I bow down toward your holy temple
and give thanks to your name,
for your love and faithfulness,
for your word which exceeds everything.

You answered me when I called;
you restored my soul and made me strong.
O Lord, all kings on earth will give you praise,
when they have heard your words.

They will celebrate the ways of the Lord,
"Great is the glory of the Lord!"
From above, the Lord watches over the lowly;
from afar, he marks down the haughty.

If I walk in the midst of trouble,
you give me life.
With outstretched arm, you save me
from the wrath of my foes,
with your right hand you deliver me.

How the Lord cares for me!
Your kindness, O Lord, endures forever.
Forsake not the work of your hands.

Glory to the Father, the Son, and the
Holy Spirit, both now and forever. Amen

ANTIPHON

SCRIPTURE
*(Read the following gospel or a gospel selection
from pages 16-23.)*

> While they were eating, Jesus took bread, said
> a blessing and broke it, and gave it to his dis-
> ciples saying, "Take and eat; this is my body."
> Then he took a cup and gave thanks, and
> passed it to them saying, "Drink this, all of
> you, for this is my blood, the blood of the
> Covenant, which is poured out for many for

the forgiveness of sins. Yes, I say to you: I will not taste the fruit of the vine from now until the day I drink new wine with you in my Father's kingdom."

Matthew 26:26-29, CCB

CLOSING PRAYER

Merciful God,
we stop in the middle of this day
to give you praise and glory.
Bless us and the work we do.
May we be instruments of your peace and love.
Grant this through Christ our Lord. Amen

Evening Prayer

For Mondays, Wednesdays, and Fridays

V. God, come to my assistance.
R. Lord, make haste to help me.
V. Glory to the Father, the Son, and the Holy Spirit,
R. Both now and forever. Amen

Hymn

(Optional. See page 67-74.)

PSALM 119

Antiphon: Know that I am with you always; yes, to the end of time.

Blessed are they whose ways are upright, who follow the law of the Lord.

Blessed are they who treasure his word and seek him with all their heart.

They do no wrong; they walk in his ways.

You have laid down precepts to be obeyed. Oh, that my ways were steadfast in observing your statutes!

Then I would not be put to disgrace, having paid attention to all your decrees.

I will praise you with an upright spirit when I learn your just precepts by heart.

I mean to observe your commandments. Oh, never abandon me.

How can young people remain pure? By living according to your word.

I seek you with my whole heart; let me not stray from your commands.

In my heart I have kept your word, that I may not sin against my Lord.

Praise to you, O Lord; instruct me in your statutes, that with my lips I may declare all your spoken decrees.

I delight in following your laws, more so than in all riches.

I will meditate on your precepts and concentrate on your ways.

Glory to the Father, the Son, and the Holy Spirit, both now and forever. Amen

ANTIPHON

SCRIPTURE READING

The reading can be a gospel reading taken from pages 16-23 or from the liturgy of the day.

SILENT REFLECTION

CANTICLE OF MARY
(Luke 1:46-55)

My soul magnifies the Lord,
and my spirit rejoices in God my Savior,
for he has looked with favor on the lowliness
    of his servant.

Surely, from now on all generations will
    call me blessed;
for the Mighty One has done great things
    for me,
and holy is his name.

His mercy is for those who fear him
from generation to generation.
He has shown strength with his arm;
he has scattered the proud in the thoughts
    of their hearts.

He has brought down the powerful from their
    thrones,
and lifted up the lowly; he has filled the hungry
    with good things,
and sent the rich away empty.

He has helped his servant Israel,
in remembrance of his mercy,
according to the promise he made to our
    ancestors,
to Abraham and to his descendants forever.

Glory to the Father, the Son, and the Holy Spirit,
both now and forever. Amen

PRAYERS OF INTERCESSION

Lord, I thank you for all the blessings of this day.

Lord, grant your blessings this evening to all those
    who are in need.

Lord, surround me with your protection and grant
    that I may have a peaceful night.

(Pray now for your own intentions.)

THE LORD'S PRAYER

CLOSING PRAYER

Lord, may our evening prayers find favor in your sight. Help us to live our lives according to the teachings of the gospel. May we follow in the footsteps of your Son, Jesus Christ our Lord, who lives and reigns with you and the Holy Spirit, one God forever and ever. Amen

(See Seasonal Prayers, *pages 43-47, for an alternative prayer proper to the season of the year.)*

Evening Prayer

For Tuesdays, Thursdays, and Saturdays

V. God, come to my assistance.
R. Lord, make haste to help me.
V. Glory to the Father, the Son, and the Holy Spirit,
R. Both now and forever. Amen

Hymn
(Optional. See pages 67-74.)

PSALM 121

Antiphon: Come and eat my bread, drink the wine
I have prepared.

I lift up my eyes to the mountains—
from where shall come my help?
My help comes from the Lord,
maker of heaven and earth.

Will he not let your foot slip,
the one watching over you?
Will he not slumber?
No, the guardian of Israel
neither slumber nor sleeps.

The Lord is your guardian,
the Lord is at your side and you in his shade;
Sunstroke will not be for you by day,
nor the spell of the moon by night.

The Lord guards you from every evil;
he will protect your life.
The Lord watches over your coming and
going both now and forever.

Glory to the Father, the Son, and
the Holy Spirit,
both now and forever. Amen

(See pages 37-39 for Scripture, Silent Reflection,
Canticle, Prayers of Intercession, the Lord's Prayer,
and Closing Prayer.*)*

Evening Prayer

For Sundays

V. God, come to my assistance.
R. Lord, make haste to help me.
V. Glory to the Father, the Son, and the Holy Spirit,
R. Both now and forever. Amen

Hymn

(Optional. See pages 67-74.)

PSALM 122
Antiphon: Let us go to the house of the Lord.

I rejoiced with those who said to me,

"Let us go to the house of the Lord!"
And now we have set foot
within your gates, O Jerusalem!

Jerusalem, just like a city,
where everything falls into place!
There the tribes go up,
the tribes of the Lord, the assembly of Israel,
to give thanks to the Lord's name.
There stand the courts of justice
the offices of the house of David.

Pray for the peace of Jerusalem:
"May those who love you prosper!
May peace be within your walls
and security within your citadels!"

For the sake of my relatives and friends
I will say, "Peace be with you!"
For the sake of the house of our Lord,
I will pray for your good.

Glory to the Father, the Son, and the
Holy Spirit, both now and forever. Amen

ANTIPHON

(See pages 37-39 for Scripture, Silent Reflection, Canticle, Prayers of Intercession, the Lord's Prayer, *and* Closing Prayer. *See* Seasonal Prayers, *pages 43-47, for an alternative prayer proper to the season of the year.)*

Seasonal Prayers

The eucharistic sacrifice is the source and culmination of the whole Christian life. Both private and public devotion toward the Eucharist, therefore, including the devotion outside Mass, are strongly encouraged when celebrated according to the regulations of lawful authority.

In the arrangement of devotional services of this kind, the liturgical seasons should be taken into account. Devotions should be in harmony with the sacred liturgy in some sense, take their origin from the liturgy, and lead the people back to the liturgy. (See *The Constitution on the Sacred Liturgy*, 20, Chapter II, 79.)

Prayer During the Advent Season

Lord, move our hearts to prepare joyfully for the coming of Christ our Savior. Protect us from all dangers, and free our minds and hearts from the darkness that hinders your light. As we look forward to the feast of your Son's birth, increase our faith and trust in your love. We ask this through Christ our Lord. Amen

Prayer During the Christmas Season

While all was in quiet silence and the night was in the middle of its course, your almighty Word leapt down from the Royal Throne.
Wisdom 18:14-15, CCB

Lord Jesus Christ, you are present here in the Blessed Sacrament, as you were present in Bethlehem at your birth. During this season in which we celebrate your coming among us in our human flesh, fill us with faith, hope, and love. May the light of your presence shine through us in our thoughts, words, and deeds. Amen

Prayer During the Lenten Season

We adore you, Lord Jesus Christ, and we praise you, because by your holy cross you have saved the world.

Lord Jesus Christ, by your passion, death, and resurrection you have redeemed us. As we come before your eucharistic presence, strengthen and protect us from all harm. By your holy wounds, may we experience in our lives your love and mercy. Amen

Prayer During the Easter Season

V. Alleluia. Christ has become our paschal sacrifice;

R. Let us be filled with joy. Alleluia.

V. This is the day the Lord has made;

R. Let us rejoice and be glad.

Risen Jesus, fill me with the joy of your Resurrection. Surround me with the radiant light of your glory. Transform all the areas of my life that are in need of your healing touch.

Like Mary of Magdala, let me hear you whisper my name. Like the disciples on the road to Emmaus, help me to know you in the breaking of the bread, the holy Eucharist.

With Thomas, let me touch you and cry, "My Lord and my God." Risen Jesus, cover me with the radiance of your love. Let me be your messenger of peace, joy, and love to all I meet. Amen

Prayer for Pentecost

Lord Jesus Christ, your gift of the Holy Spirit dwells in us and in the whole Church. During this time of Pentecost I ask you to open my mind and heart to the anointing and power of the Holy Spirit.

Spirit of Jesus, come to me, enable me to think like Jesus Christ, to will like Jesus Christ, to act and suffer like Jesus Christ. Holy Spirit, grant that I may live my life in witness to the gospel of Jesus. Amen

Prayer for Ordinary Time

God, our Father,
you are the source of all life and goodness.
Lead us in the way of your commandments.
May we always do what pleases you,
in thought, word, and deed.
We ask this through our Lord Jesus Christ,
your Son, who lives and reigns with you
and the Holy Spirit, one God,
forever and ever. Amen

How to Make
a Holy Hour

❧

A eucharistic holy hour is nothing more—and nothing less—than spending time in the presence of Jesus in the holy Eucharist. People commonly make a half-hour visit before the Blessed Sacrament, whether reserved or exposed. A holy hour may be observed either in common or in private. Many parishes have an hour or several hours set aside for daily, weekly, or monthly public adoration of the Blessed Sacrament.

Practice of
Eucharistic Adoration

1. Find a church or chapel that has the Blessed Sacrament reserved or exposed.

2. Upon entering, genuflect or bow, then kneel or sit. Gazing on the Eucharist, make an act of adoration.
3. Turn to pages 53-55 and pray "Visits to the Most Blessed Sacrament" or any other prayer that you would like to use.

From the Writings of Saint Alphonsus Liguori on the Eucharist

Saint Alphonsus Liguori, the great doctor of prayer, has this to say about making a private visit to our Lord, present in the Blessed Sacrament:

Be also assured that Jesus Christ finds means to console a soul that remains with a recollected spirit before the Most Blessed Sacrament, far beyond what the world can do with all its feasts and pastimes. Oh, how sweet a joy it is to remain with faith and tender devotion before an altar, and converse familiarly with Jesus Christ, who is there for the express purpose of listening to and graciously hearing those who pray to him; to ask his pardon for the displeasures which we have caused him; to represent our wants to him, as a friend does to a friend in whom he places all his confidence; to ask him for his graces, for his love, and for his kingdom; but above all to remain in his presence making acts of love toward the Lord who is on the very altar praying to the Eternal Father for us, and is there burning with love for us.

The Holy Eucharist

To sum up Saint Alphonsus' suggestion:

1. Place yourself in the presence of Jesus in the Blessed Sacrament.
2. Speak with Jesus Christ present before you as you would speak to a friend.
3. Ask forgiveness of your sins and faults.
4. Tell Jesus of your needs.
5. Ask Jesus for greater love of him and your neighbor.
6. Remain in his eucharistic presence praying prayers of love.

You must also be aware, that in a quarter of an hour's prayer spent in the presence of the Blessed Sacrament, you will perhaps gain more than in all the other spiritual exercise of the day. It is true that in every place God graciously hears the petitions of those who pray to him, having promised to do so. "Ask, and you shall receive," says Jesus Christ.

The Holy Eucharist

Spiritual Communion is also a practice of eucharistic adoration. Saint Alphonsus writes

A spiritual communion, according to Saint Thomas, consists in an ardent desire to receive Jesus in the Most Holy Sacrament, and in lovingly embracing him as if we had actually received him. All those who desire to advance in the love of Jesus Christ are exhorted to make a spiritual Communion at least once in every visit that they pay to the Most Blessed Sacrament. This devotion is far more profitable than some suppose, and at the same time nothing can be easier to practice.

The Holy Eucharist

Act of Spiritual Communion

Lord Jesus Christ,
I believe that you are present,
body, blood, soul, and divinity,
in the sacrament of the Eucharist.
I love you and desire you.
Come into my heart. I embrace you.
Never let me be parted from your love.
Amen

Devotional Prayers to Jesus Present in the Blessed Sacrament

Visits to the Most Blessed Sacrament by Saint Alphonsus

My Lord Jesus Christ, I believe that you are really here in this sacrament. Night and day you remain here compassionate and loving. You call, you wait for, you welcome everyone who comes to visit you.

Unimportant though I am, I adore you. I thank you for all the wonderful graces you have given me. But thank you especially for having given me yourself in this sacrament, for having asked your own Mother to mother me, for having called me here to talk to you.

I am here before you today to do three things: to thank you for these precious gifts, to make up for all the disrespect that you receive in this sacrament from those who offend you, to adore you everywhere in the world where you are present in this living bread but are left abandoned and unloved.

My Jesus, I love you with all my heart. I know I have displeased you often in the past—I am sorry. With your help I promise never to do it again. I am only a miserable sinner, but I consecrate myself to you completely. I give you my will, my love, my desires, everything I own. From now on do what you please with me. All I ask is that you love me, that you keep me faithful to the end of my life. I ask for the grace to do your will exactly as you want it done.

I pray for the souls in purgatory—especially for those who were close to you in this sacrament and close to your Mother Mary. I pray for every soul hardened in sin. My Savior, I unite my love to the love of your divine heart, and I offer this offering in your name. Amen

Spiritual Communion

(to be said after each visit)

My Jesus, I believe you are really here in the Blessed Sacrament. I love you more than anything in the world, and I hunger to receive your Body and Blood. But since I cannot receive Communion at this moment, feed my soul at least spiritually. I unite myself to you now as I do when I actually receive you. Never let me drift away from you. Amen

(A Scripture reading is suggested from pages 16-23.)

Prayers from the Heart

O my beloved Jesus, O God, who has loved me with love exceeding! What more can you do to make yourself loved by ungrateful people? If we loved you, all the churches would be continually filled with people prostrate on the ground adoring and thanking you, burning with love for you, and seeing you with the eyes of faith, hidden in a tabernacle. But no, we are forgetful of you and your love. We are ready enough to try to win the favor of a person from whom we hope for some miserable advantage, while we leave you, Lord, abandoned and alone. If only by my devotion I could make reparation for such ingratitude! I am sorry that I also have been careless and ungrateful. In the future I will change my ways, I will devote myself to your service as much as possible. Inflame me with your holy love, so that from this day forward I may live only to love and to please you. You deserve the love of all hearts. If at one time I have despised you, I now desire nothing but to love you. O my Jesus, you are my love and my only good, "my God and my all."

Most Holy Virgin Mary, obtain for me, I pray, a great love for the Most Holy Sacrament.

Prayer of Adoration

I adore you Jesus, true God, and true man, present in the holy Eucharist, kneeling before you and united in spirit with all the faithful on earth and all the saints in heaven. In gratitude for so great a blessing, I love you with all my heart, for you are worthy of all praise and adoration.

Lord Jesus Christ, may I never offend you with my lack of love. May your eucharistic presence refresh me in body and soul. Mary, Mother of the eucharistic Lord, pray for me and obtain for me a greater love for Jesus. Amen

Prayer to Jesus in the Holy Eucharist

My Lord Jesus Christ, Your eucharistic presence teaches me how to love as you have loved me.

In your great love for me you continue to give yourself, body, blood, soul, and divinity in this sacrament of your love.

As I pray here in your eucharistic presence, enkindle in me the fire of your gospel. Nourish me with your love and compassion, so that I may be your living presence to all I meet. Amen

Short Prayers to the Eucharistic Heart of Jesus

The following short prayers are prayed slowly, pausing after words and phrases. Allow the Lord Jesus, present before you in the Eucharist, to bring you into silent prayer. It is not necessary to pray all of them. Remember, prayer before the eucharistic Lord draws us into the silent depth of mystery. Give the Lord some time to respond to your prayers. Silence in his presence is the greatest prayer.

I.

Eucharistic Heart of Jesus,
Fill my heart with that same love
that burned in your heart.
May I become love and mercy

to those who live in pain and suffering.
May I become the living gospel
of your compassionate love.

II.

Eucharistic Heart of Jesus,
Fill me with faith, hope, and love.
When I find myself lacking in charity,
help me to see your presence
in those around me.
Increase my faith
when I find it hard to understand.
Give me hope when life around me
seems empty and forsaken.
May your presence
in the Blessed Sacrament of the altar
be my courage and strength.

III.

Eucharistic Heart of Jesus,
Your gift of the holy Eucharist
strengthens me on the journey of life.
Transform me into your disciple and
    send me

to those who are in need of your love.
May I be your hands to those who are
    helpless.
May I be your heart to those who are
    unloved.
Surround me with your light and allow me
to be an instrument of your peace and joy.

IV.

Eucharistic Heart of Jesus,
Many times I find life to be difficult
and filled with anxiety.
Help me in times of uncertainty
to come into your eucharistic presence.
Be my strength, my rock, my fortress,
    and my refuge.
Help me, by the power of your Holy Spirit,
to feel the light of your Resurrection
surrounding me and protecting me from
    all danger.
In you I hope, Lord; may I never be
    disappointed.

Prayers After Mass

Prayer to Jesus Christ, Crucified

Behold, my beloved and good Jesus. I cast myself upon my knees in your sight, and with the most fervent desire of my soul I pray and beseech you to impress upon my heart lively sentiments of faith, hope, and charity, with true repentance for my sins and a most firm desire of amendment; while with deep affection and grief of soul I consider within myself and mentally contemplate your five most precious wounds, having before my eyes that which David the prophet long ago spoke about you, my Jesus: "They have pierced my hands and my feet; I can count all my bones" (see Psalm 22:16-17).

Anima Christi

Soul of Christ, sanctify me.
Body of Christ, save me.
Blood of Christ, inebriate me.
Water from the side of Christ, wash me.
Passion of Christ, strengthen me.
O good Jesus, hear me.
Within your wounds hide me.

Never let me be separated from you.
From the evil one protect me.
At the hour of my death call me,
And bid me come to you,
That with your saints I may praise you
Forever and ever. Amen

Prayer of Saint Francis of Assisi

Lord, make me an instrument of your peace.
Where there is hatred, let me sow love;
Where there is injury, pardon;
Where there is doubt, faith;
Where there is despair, hope;
Where there is darkness, light;
And where there is sadness, joy.

O Divine Master, grant that I may not so much seek
to be consoled as to console; to be understood as to
understand; to be loved as to love. For it is in giving that we receive, it is in pardoning that we are
pardoned, and it is in dying that we are born to eternal life. Amen

Prayer Recited by Pope John XXIII

I believe, Lord, but let me believe more firmly; I hope, but let me hope more confidently; I love, but let me love more ardently; I sorrow, but let me sorrow more strongly.

Lord, this is my prayer: may you enlighten my mind, inflame my will, cleanse my heart, sanctify my soul. Direct me by your wisdom, surround me by your justice, comfort me by your mercy, protect me by your power. Let me weep for my past sins; let me repel future temptations.

Let me correct my evil inclinations; let me cultivate my proper virtues. Make me prudent in judgment, steadfast in danger, patient in adversity, humble in my decisions.

Let me conquer pleasure by austerity, greediness by generosity, anger by mildness, tepidity by fervor.

Grant, Lord, that I may be attentive in prayer, moderate in my sustenance, diligent in my work, firm in my decisions.

Let me learn from you how fragile is the earthly, how great the divine, how brief the temporal, how permanent the eternal.

Grant that I may prepare for death, fear judgment, escape hell, and obtain paradise, through Christ our Lord. Amen

Prayer of Saint Columba

Lord, grant me, I pray you, in the name of Jesus Christ, your Son, my God, the love that does not fail, so that my lamp may be always lighted, never extinguished, and may burn for me and give light to others. Christ, kindle our lamps, that they may always shine in your temple and continually receive light from you, the Light Eternal, that our own darkness may be illuminated and the darkness of the world expelled from us. Give my lamp such a share of your light that its brightness may reveal to me the Holy of Holies, where you are the eternal priest. May I love and contemplate you alone and may my lamp ever burn and shine before you.

Most loving Savior, show yourself to us who seek you, so that knowing you we may love you alone, desire you alone, contemplate you alone by day and night and keep you always in our thoughts. May affection for you pervade our hearts. May attachment to you take possession of us. May love of you fill all our senses. May we know no other love except you who are Eternal. Lord Jesus Christ, to you be glory forever and ever. Amen

Prayers to Be Said Throughout the Day

Prayer to Christ

Christ, yesterday and today,
the beginning and the end,
the Alpha and the Omega.
All time belongs to him,
and all ages;
to him be glory and power
through every age forever. Amen

Three Brief Prayers

Lord Jesus Christ, by your holy and
glorious wounds, have mercy on us.

∽∾

My Lord and my God!

∽∾

My God and my all!

Prayer to Mary

Blessed Virgin Mary,
You were chosen by the Father to be the
    mother of his Son,
Our Lord Jesus Christ.
Your acceptance of the Word Incarnate
    brings joy to the whole church,
and salvation for the whole world.
Through your prayers
    obtain for us a deeper love for the mystery
    of the Eucharist.
May our devotion to the Lord Jesus Christ,
    present in the sacrament of his love,
    bring us one day to share in the heavenly banquet.
Mary, Mother of Christ, intercede for us.
Amen

Hymns

O Living Bread from Heaven

O living bread from heaven, How well
you fed your guest!
The gifts that you have given Have filled
my heart with rest.
O wondrous food of blessing, O cup that
heals our woes,
My heart, this gift possessing, With
praises overflows!

You gave me all I wanted This food can
death destroy:
And you have freely granted The cup of
endless joy.
O Lord, I do not merit The favor you
have shown,

And all my soul and spirit Bow down
  before your throne.

Text: Wie wohl has du gelabet, Johann Rist, 1607-1667, in
Sabbahtische Seelenlust, 1651, tr. by Catherine Winkworth,
1827-1878, in her *Lyra Germanica II*, 1858, alt.
Tune: Samuel Sebastian Wesley, 1810-1876, in Kemble's
Selection of Psalms and Hymns, 1864.
AURELIA 7.6.7.6 D* —tune "The Church's One Foundation."

Alleluia! Sing to Jesus!

Alleluia! Sing to Jesus! His the scepter,
  his the throne;
Alleluia! His the triumph, his the victory
  alone:
Hark! The songs of peaceful Zion thunder
  like a mighty flood:
Jesus out of every nation has redeemed us
  by his blood.

Alleluia! Bread of angels, and on earth
  our food, our stay.
Alleluia! Here the sinful flee to you from
  day to day.
Intercessor, friend of sinners, earth's
  Redeemer plead for me,

Where the songs of all the sinless sweep
across the crystal sea.

Alleluia! King eternal, you the Lord of
lords we own;
Alleluia! Born of Mary, earth your
footstool, heav'n your throne:
You within the veil have entered, robed
in flesh, our great high priest:
You on earth both priest and victim in the
eucharistic feast.

Text: William Chaterton Dix, 1837-1898, in his *Altar
Songs, Verses On the Holy Eucharist,* 1867, alt.
Tune: Composed in 1830 by Rowland Hugh Prichard,
1811-1887, in Griffith Robert's *Haleliwiah Drachefn,* 1855.
HYFRYDL 8.7.8.7 D

Let All Mortal Flesh
Keep Silence

Let all mortal flesh keep silence, and with
fear and trembling stand:
Ponder nothing earthly minded for with
blessing in his hand

Christ our God to earth descendeth,
  our full homage to demand.

King of kings, yet born of Mary, as of old
  on earth he stood,
Lord of lords in human vesture, in the
  Body and the Blood
He will give to all the faithful his own
  self for heav'nly food.

Rank on rank the host of heaven spreads
  its vanguard on the way,
As the Light of Light descendeth from the
  realms of endless day,
That the pow'rs of hell may vanish as the
  darkness clears away.

At his feet the sixwinged seraph,
  Cherubim with sleepless eye,
Veil their faces to the presence as with
  ceaseless voice they cry,
"Alleluia, Alleluia, Alleluia,
  Lord most high!"

Text: Greek: Eigesato pasa sarx broteia, *Liturgy of St. James*, 5th century, para. by Gerard Moultrie, 1829-1885, in Orbey Shipley's *Lyra Eucharistica*, 1864.

Tune: Trad. French choral melody, 17th century, from *Chansons Populaires des Provinces de France*, IV, 1860, acc. by Russell Woollen, 1980.
PICARDY 8.7.8.7.8.7

Holy God, We Praise Thy Name

Holy God, we praise thy Name; Lord of
all, we bow before thee!
All on earth thy sceptre claim, all in
heav'n above adore thee;
Infinite thy vast domain, everlasting is
thy reign.

Hark! the loud celestial hymn angel
choirs above are raising,
Cherubim and seraphim, in unceasing
chorus praising;
Fill the heav'ns with sweet accord: Holy,
holy, holy Lord.

Holy Father, Holy Son, Holy Spirit, Three
we name thee;

While in essence only One, undivided
  God we claim thee;
And adoring bend the knee, while we
  own the mystery.

Text: Latin: Te Deum laudamus; German: Grosser Gott, wir loben
dich, Ignaz Franz, 1719-1790, in *Katholisches Gesangbuch,*
Vienna, c.1774, tr. by Clarence Alphonsus Walworth, 1820-1900,
in Catholic Psalmist, 1858.
Tune: Melody adapted from *Katholisches Gesangbuch,* Vienna,
c.1774.
GROSSER GOTT (Te Deum) 7.8.7.8.77

O God of Loveliness

O God of loveliness, O Lord of heav'n
  above,
How worthy to possess my heart's
  devoted love!
So sweet thy countenance, so gracious
  to behold
That one, one only glance to me were
  bliss untold!

Thou art blest Three in One, yet
  undivided still.
Thou art that One alone whose love my
  heart can fill.

The heav'ns, the earth below were
  fashioned by thy word;
How amiable art thou, my ever
  dearest Lord!

To think thou art my God! O thought for
  ever blest!
My heart has overflow'd with joy within
  my breast;
My soul so full of bliss is plunged
  as in a sea,
Deep in the sweet abyss of holy charity.

Text: Obello Dio, Signot del Paradiso, St. Alphonsus Liguori, 1696-1787, tr. by Edmund Vaughan, C.Ss.R., 1827-1908, in his *Works*, 1863.
Tune: Silesian melody, for Schlesische Volkslieder, Leipzig, 1842, alt.
ST. ELIZABETH (Ascalon) 12 12.12 12

Crown Him with Many Crowns

Crown him with many crowns, the Lamb
upon his throne;
Hark! how the heav'nly anthem drowns
all music but its own:
Awake my soul, and sing, he died to set
us free;
Now hail him as your glorious king
through all eternity.

Crown him the Son of God before all
worlds began:
And you who tread where he has trod
crown him the Son of man;
Who every grief has known that wrings
the human breast,
And takes and bears them for his own
that all in him may rest.

Text: Based on Revelation 19:12; Matthew Bridges, 1800-1894,
in his *Hymns of the Heart,* 2nd ed., 1851, and Godfrey Thring,
1823-1903, in his *Hymns & Sacred Lyrics,* 1874, alt.
Tune: Georg Job Elvey, 1816-1893, in *Hymns Ancient and
Modern,* 1868.
DIADEMATA S.M.D

Church Teaching on the Eucharist

These reflections, taken from the *Catechism of the Catholic Church (CCC)* and *The Constitution on the Sacred Liturgy,* offer us a firm foundation on which to build our experience of eucharistic adoration.

> The wonderful works of God among the people of the Old Testament were but a prelude to the work of Christ the Lord in redeeming mankind and giving perfect glory to God. He accomplished this work principally by the Paschal mystery of his blessed Passion, Resurrection from the dead, and glorious Ascension, whereby "dying he destroyed our death, rising he restored our life." For it was from

the side of Christ as he slept the sleep of death upon the cross that there came forth "the wondrous sacrament of the whole Church." For this reason, the Church celebrates in the liturgy above all the Paschal mystery by which Christ accomplished the work of our salvation.

CCC, #1067

The mode of Christ's presence under the Eucharistic species is unique. It raises the Eucharist above all the sacraments as "the perfection of the spiritual life and the end to which all the sacraments tend." In the most blessed sacrament of the Eucharist "the body and blood, together with the soul and divinity, of our Lord Jesus Christ and, therefore, the whole Christ is truly, really and substantially contained." "This presence is called 'real'—by which is not intended to exclude the other types of presence as if they could not be 'real' too, but because it is presence in the fullest sense: that is to say, it is a substantial presence by which Christ, God and man, makes himself wholly and entirely present."

CCC, #1374

The Council of Trent summarizes the Catholic faith by declaring: "Because Christ our Redeemer said that it was truly his body that he was offering under the species of bread, it has always been the conviction of the Church of God, and this holy Council declares it again, that by the consecration of the bread and wine there takes place a change of the whole substance of the bread into the substance of the body of Christ our Lord and of the whole substance of wine into the substance of his blood. This change the holy Catholic Church has fittingly and properly called transubstantiation."

CCC, #1376

In the liturgy of the Mass we express our faith in the real presence of Christ under the species of bread and wine by, among other ways, genuflecting or bowing deeply as a sign of adoration of the Lord. "The Catholic Church has always offered and still offers to the sacrament of the Eucharist the cult of adoration, not only during Mass, but also outside of it, reserving the consecrated hosts with the utmost care, exposing them to the solemn veneration of the faithful, and carrying them in procession."

CCC, #1378

The tabernacle was first intended for the reservation of the Eucharist in a worthy place so that it could be brought to the sick and those absent, outside of Mass. As faith in the real presence of Christ in his Eucharist deepened, the Church became conscious of the meaning of silent adoration of the Lord present under the Eucharistic species. It is for this reason that the tabernacle should be located in an especially worthy place in the church and should be constructed in such a way that it emphasizes and manifests the truth of the real presence of Christ in the Blessed Sacrament.

CCC, #1379

Let them remember also that by prayer of this kind before Christ in the Blessed Sacrament they prolong that union which they have achieved with him in Holy Communion, and renew the covenant which commits them to practice in their lives and conduct what they have received in faith in the celebration of the Eucharist and in the reception of the Sacrament. Let them strive, therefore, to live their whole lives joyously in the strength of this heavenly food, participating in the death and resurrection of the Lord. Each individual, therefore, should be eager to do good works and to please God, making it his aim to impregnate the world with the Christian spirit and to be a faithful witness to Christ in all things in the midst of human society.

From *The Constitution on the Sacred Liturgy,* Chapter II, #81, "On Holy Communion and Worship of the Eucharistic Mystery Outside of Mass," in *Vatican Council II: The Conciliar and Post Conciliar Documents,* Austin Flannery, O.P., General Editor. Costello Publishing Co., Northport, NY. 1987.

Going Forth

❦

Go, therefore, and make disciples from all nations. Baptize them in the Name of the Father and of the Son and of the Holy Spirit, and teach them to fulfill all that I have commanded you. I am with you always until the end of this world.

Matthew 28:19-20, CCB

Lord Jesus Christ, I have spent this time of adoration and prayer in your eucharistic presence. Fill my life with love, joy, peace, and kindness. Transform me by the power of your Holy Spirit into a living image of your compassionate presence. For we are "children of light and of the day" (1 Thessalonians 5:5), called to preach the gospel to all lands. May I go forth from this hour of adoration and prayer to be your hands, feet, and heart to all those I meet. Risen Jesus, may I be surrounded by the radiance of your love. Amen